WHEN DADDY COMES HOME

WHEN DADDY COMES HOME

MAGGIE HUNDSHAMER

Illustrated by Micaela Stéfano

When Daddy Comes Home

For information about this title or to order other books and/or electronic media, contact the publisher:

Maggie Hundshamer/EGA Publishing
Fairfield, CA
Vetcomeshome@gmail.com

ISBNs:
Hardcover: 978-0-9978595-0-8
Softcover: 978-0-9978595-2-2
Ebooks (Kindle and ePub): 978-0-9978595-1-5

Illustrated by Micaela Stéfano
Cover and interior design: 1106 Design, LLC (www.1106design.com)

To Josh and Bella:

Thank you for being proud

no matter what,

you save me every day.

My daddy loves me,
this I don't doubt.
But sometimes he has trouble
getting his feelings out.

You see, my daddy is a Veteran
and he went away.
He stayed in the desert
to keep the bad guys at bay.

He missed me a lot,
and I missed him too.
It was a long time apart
that we had to go through.

When Daddy came home,
I was so overjoyed!
I laughed so loud
showing him all of my toys.

USA

When Daddy smiled back,
he looked very sad.
I didn't know what was wrong,
and I thought I'd been bad.

I gave him a hug,
and my daddy cried.
"I'm so happy baby,
to be here by your side."

USO

He sat me down
and began to explain,
why when he came home
he just wasn't the same.

"Daddy loves you,
and I'm happy to be home.
I hated to go
and leave you all alone."

"Daddy's work was real hard,
and I had to be tough.
I carried your picture
and some days that was enough."

#1
DAD

"I want you to know,
that sometimes I'm sad.
It's not you my sweet baby,
you haven't been bad."

"Daddy heard lots of loud noises,
and I saw some very bad things.
Some of my friends
went to heaven with wings."

#1
DAD

"There are days that I miss them,
and those days are rough.
I'm going to need you to help me,
I need you to be tough."

"Sometimes Daddy has nightmares
like you used to do.
Just tell me it's okay,
like I used to tell you."

"Hold my hand tight
and I won't be scared.
I know that I'm home,
and I know that you care."

"Daddy flinches at loud noises,
so try to understand.
That super loud screaming
puts shakes in my hands."

"Some days Daddy needs naps,
my body feels tired.
So snuggles with Daddy
are now required."

“We can do this together,
just me and you.
You help take care of me,
and I’ll help take care of you.”

I hugged my dad tight
and whispered in his ear.
"I love you, Daddy,
and I'll always be here."

Acknowledgments and special thanks go to the following individuals and companies for their continued support in the making of this book. Without their time and generosity you would not be reading it today.

HOBART JAYCEES INC. (www.hobartjaycees.com)
Allowing young people to learn while giving back

Drew Cope, lifestyle trainer (www.VeteransWelcome.com)
Supporting heroes' physical, emotional and financial health through superior nutrition

Ben Gottlieb and Aaron Hart (www.the5b.com)
Providing humor to veterans everywhere by taking real-world issues lightly and building a community of brotherhood similar to active duty units

The silent professionals at Veteran Syndicate Radio (www.VetRS.com)
The #1 veteran-owned radio network

Mike Friedmann at Fallen Hero Bracelets (www.fallenherobracelets.com)
Honoring those who gave all

Chelsea Firearms LLC (www.chelseafirearmscompany.com)
Firearm sales and repair for military and police officers

Leigh and Bloo (www.leighandbloo.com)
Model/photographer/veteran advocate and lifestyle motivator: Columbia, South Carolina

T-Rex Arms, LLC Gun Range (734-325-7898)
Firing range catering to veterans and the community: Belleville, Michigan

Lawrence Dennis, Hardcore Anglers (www.hardcoreanglers.com)
Veteran owned, offering discounts and free fishing for disabled veterans

Chad and Jennifer Underwood (www.shuckinggoodtime.com)
You pick your setting, we discover your pearl, guaranteed!

Pennsylvania Security Training Institute (www.psti.biz/866-260-5285)
Law enforcement training and civilian defense: Uniontown, Pennsylvania

Matthew Sharon (210-867-6419)
Aspiring racer, Sgtgrogg Adventures

1106 Design, LLC (1106design.com)
Book design and indie-publishing advice, with hand-holding

Brian D. Wolfe AMS3(AW) USN, Brian Hundshamer, Bonnie Marais, Patrolman Kat Maggiulli, Aaron Moshier, The Chaney Family, The Carson Family, Andrew Dudek, Alexis Perez, Jessica Strohl, Rebecca Corey, Teddy Byrd, Devon Miller, Ryan Loya, Danny Maher, Mike Cruz, and Zach Ferguson.

In memory of

all the men and women

who gave their all

for our freedom.

About the Author

Maggie Hundshamer is a United States Marine Corps veteran currently living in southern California. She is a former 6153 Airframes Mechanic previously attached to HMH 464.

To contact the author, email
vetcomeshome@gmail.com

Semper Fidelis

Made in the USA
Lexington, KY
12 September 2016